Heart
Whispers

Heart Whispers

POEMS

Locke Rush, PhD

Ilm House-LLC
Unionville, PA

Library of Congress Control Number: 2019907848
ISBN-978-0-9726607-2-3

Copyright ©2019 by Ilm House-LLC
Box 535, Unionville, PA 19375

Copyright ©2019 by Locke Rush
All rights reserved. Nor portion of this book may be reproduced in any manner without written permission from the publisher.

Contents

Part One

The Butterfly   1
Thy Wonders – A Prayer   2
Love Knot Earrings   3
The Purple River Man   3
The Monastery   4
Poem Mania   4
The Visitor   5
The Shopkeeper   6
Habits   7
The Beggar   8
Grace   9
The Mime   10
Making Tea   11
Fig Tree   12
Good and Evil   13
The Veg Lady   14
Children Know   15
Angels   16
Elusive Butterfly of Love   17
The Wise Ones   18
Silence   19
Wild Turkey   20
Twilight   21
Wise Child   22
The Beast   23
Patience   24
Thoughts on the Cruise Ship   25

The Revolution   26
The Invisible One   27
A Strange Fellow, This Mind   28
Follies   29
Cruise Stop   30
Eyes   31
Smiles   32
A Summer Cruise   33
Leaving   34
The Campo   35
Siena   36
The Piazza   37
Home Away From Home   38
Barking Dogs   39
Winding Way   40
Blackberry Bush   41
What a Lovely Room   42
How Do We Proceed?   43
Taming the Beast   44
Another Quiet Day   45
We Got Lost   46
The Museum   47
The Point   48
At the Window   49
What Can We Do?   50
Going Home   51
Cleaning the Spot   52

(Continued on next page)

Part Two

The Flower   55
Territory   56
Sharks   57
Expediency   58
Habits   59
The Beholder   60
The Compass   61
The Snow Goose   62
The Fig Tree   63
Learning   64
The Flashlight   65
Students   66
The Seed   67
The Movie   68
Hero Fish   69
What Is The Use?   70
A Light   71
The Surgeon   72
Difficulty   73
Essence   74
The Prism   75
Stains   76
Duty   77
Belief   78
Who Am I?   79
Dogs   80
Noah   81
Nests   82
Clowns   83
Effort   84
Teacher   85
Destruction   86
Seed   87
Heart   88
Dying   89
What Is It?   90
The Veil   91

Heaven & Hell   92
Marriage   93
Not So Long Ago   94
Things of Value   95
My Cat   96
Movies   97
Storm   98
How?   99
We Must Not Stop   100
Sirens in the Night   101
Interpreter   102
Home   103
Honey   104
Pure Color   105
Taproot   106
Harvest   107
Sleep   108
Zikr   109
Japanese Beetles   110
Lions   111
Pictures   112
Heart & Mind   113
Net   114
Burdens   115
The Boat   116
Habits   117
Adam   118
LSD   119
My Walk   120
Dog   121
Why?   122
Jihad   123
Satan   124
My Friend   125
What Are We to Do?   126
Our Classroom   127
Anger   128
The Posse   129
Artichoke   130

The Water of Our Soul   131
The Squirrel   132
What Worry?   133
Aging   134
Hurrying   135
Dream   136
The U.S.A.   137
My Best Friends   138
Determination   139
Arch   140
Minkie   141
Alexander   142
Echoes   143

Sleep   144
Tea   145
Spotless   146
Tricks   147
My elbow   148
Hastiness   149
Penmanship   150
Sex   151
The Mirror   152
Poetry   153
Here Today   154
Trees   155
The Dog   156

Part Three

What Is It?   158
The Path   159
Walking   160
Humility   161
Surrender   162
The Little Boy   163
Forgiveness   164
The Tailor   165
The Dog   166
Night Blooming Sirius   167
Faults   168
The Ant   169
The Funeral   170
Snow Geese   171
Seeds   172
Hummingbird   173
A Dog   174
Cleaning the Pot   175
The Footrace   176
Getting There is the Fun   177
The Carver   178
Don't Bite a Dog   179

Making Tea   180
Balance   181
Compost   182
What We Have   183
Morning Walk   184
My Finger   185
Quicksilver   186
Getting Angry   187
The Oyster   188
The Fig Tree   189
Skins   190
Salt   191
Incense   192
The Child Knows   193
Let Go   194
Humility   195
Image   196
Traveler   197
The Tail   198
Tiger Taming   199
The Rooster   200
Enyatta's Necklace   201

(Continued on next page)

Part Three (Continued)

The Garland   202
Light   203
Bad Dream   204
Idol Worship   205
The Bumblebee   206
Flying   207
Medicines   208
Faith   209
Woodworking   210
Beating an Orange   211
Outer Church   212
Fragrance   213
Rivers   214
Bird Nests   215
Fishing   216
The Therapist   217
Washing Machines   218
Covers   219
Kites   220
Movie House   221
The Well   222
Snipping   223
My Friend   224
Understanding   225
Instinct   226
The Cover   227
White   228
Airplanes   229
Mimosa   230
The Key   231

M. R. BAWA MUHAIYADDEEN

In Japan, in the nineteen sixties, I first began to write down the thoughts and images that came from my heart. They flowed out of me easily and seemed to have a certain spiritual tone and meaning.

Some years later, after meeting Bawa Muhaiyaddeen, these poems came more frequently and clearly and touched more deeply my being and the meaning of my life. A few years ago, I gathered them all together and they became *Heart Whispers*. May these words help to bring understanding and peace into our hearts.

Locke Rush

Part One

THE BUTTERFLY

'Tis a Monarch
but a frail one
that you could crush
twixt your fingers.

Yet it flies
thousands of miles
miles above the earth,
riding the crest of storms
that would crush
a larger traveler.

Arriving at its destination
it sips delicately
the nectar of God.
What a wonder!

Such a mystery,
this butterfly.

THY WONDERS – A PRAYER

On this spring day, oh Lord,
let my heart be warmed by the sun
and my senses awakened
by the splendor and beauty
of Thy creations.

But, oh Lord,
let these myriad wonders
serve as reminders
of the wonders of the soul
and the Path of Righteousness.

Let their beauty serve not
to captivate my senses,
but let the bird's song
the sun's warmth
the flowers' fragrance
speak of Thy wonder,
that we may praise and honor
Thy Spirit through
these creations.

LOVE KNOT EARRINGS

So small, shining, and lovely
are the strands which
bind the love knot.

So dutiful, patient, and loving
are the qualities which
nourish our union.

So pure, transcendent, resplendent
are the gifts from God
which grace
our daily lives.

THE PURPLE RIVER MAN

Here's to the Purple River Man:
He's been everywhere;
he looks as though
he might explode --
but that's his color.

THE MONASTERY

At Dawn
eating rice
I see tears
in a monk's eye.

POEM MANIA

The road shall be
neither good nor bad.
It will cut across
the country:
not a straight way
but connecting all byways
so that one may meet
all strangers
and all strangers – one.

THE VISITOR

She came out of the vineyard,
tail between her legs,
quivering from the sound
of guns.

We stroked her quietly
and gave her food
and water
until she was calm.

After a while
she began to play
and her true nature
came forth.

What sweetness in an animal;
what gentleness
and kind eyes
that trusted.

Sometimes she quivered
at the distant sound of a gun

But mostly she forgot
and became happy again,
greeting us each morning
with wagging tail.

Then her owner came
one evening to take her back.
He had tears in his eyes
when he saw her.

And she was gone.

THE SHOPKEEPER

The woman in the shop was short,
dark hair, full figure, and eyes
that laughed as she talked.

All around us were
fragrances, incense
and sweet-smelling soaps.

We looked for a while
and picked something
special for a friend.

The woman wrapped it,
talking all the time
as if we were old friends.

We left with our purchase
but the best fragrance
we left behind in the store:

That pure sweetness and joy
which came from
the woman.

HABITS

Isn't it strange
how we continue each day

Doing the habits
we've learned over the years?

Have you ever tried
to break a habit?

It's quite hard.

Something inside resists you –
it is unyielding

And very clever.

Once I broke an old habit
I'd had for years.

I had tried many times before
but this time it disappeared.

Of course I had a drop
of the elixir of grace –

Which removed all obstacles.

Otherwise I would still
be struggling.

THE BEGGAR

She sat on the pavement
in front of the church

An old woman with dark
and wrinkled skin

With a sign saying,
In God's name –
I am hungry.

She said nothing – only
stared ahead.

Passersby slowed –
some came to her and
dropped
a coin.

Life flowed past
and around her
as a small river.

Occasionally she would
shift her legs – look around
to see who was watching

And count her coins.

She went away for a few hours –
probably for lunch.

She's not hungry now
but the sign still stands.

It's hard work being
a beggar.

GRACE

The Tao says, "The noble man
changes slowly, like a lion.

Never trust sudden change."

Once in a while I see a glimmer
of light coming through

But mostly it is grey
and unchanging.

One day I found a tiny
green sprout:

It was a sign of hope
something was happening.

The force within is momentous,
quiet and steady;

It will surface in its own time –
usually where we don't expect it

As if to remind us
it's there,

Lest we forget:
it brings forth small miracles.

How else
could this happen?

THE MIME

He stood on a small crate –
white-faced and sad.

His pose was beseeching:
hands outstretched,

Head tilted as if to say,
come here and look at me.

He was mimicking a statue,
but he moved;

He's new at this.

After a time a child
put a coin in his plate

And his whitened face smiled
and he did a little dance

And ended with his
head cocked again.

The child was delighted
but most passers-by hardly
noticed.

Isn't it strange how
we don't see?

Perhaps it's too much
like reality.

MAKING TEA

I've been making tea for years,
enjoying that first taste,

Yet each time
it's different.

I never know exactly
how it will taste.

Sometimes I'm surprised
and pleased at its fragrance;

Other times it's just tea.

You'd think after all these years
I'd get it right.

But making tea is an art
and must be practiced carefully:

The kind of water, the amount,
the temperature, the steeping time
Can vary slightly,
and the result is different.

We are like this: Inherent
inside is the fragrance.

But how we prepare it,
with wisdom and care and
patience,

Is most important
for the taste.

FIG TREE

It was a wet summer:
plants grew large

And the fig tree near our house
was heavy.

I never saw
such big fruits

But no one
was picking them.

So they split themselves
wide open

For passers-by to see
the red fruit inside.

Even then
no one came

Except the bees
and insects.

Isn't it a wonder
how we miss
what God serves us?

GOOD AND EVIL

We are told that
God's kingdom contains
both good and evil

And that He allows evil –
that it has a value.

For how else could we know
good?

I know it's all about choice,
but
isn't there an easier way?

THE VEG LADY

The jolly lady
in the vegetable store
laughed easily
but had sad eyes.

She showed us
a tiny silver frame
of a young man.

She'd lost her son
a few years back
and you could tell
it was still there:
the sadness, wonder, and hope.

Her store was full of
wondrous fruits and vegetables
and she laughed
and joked with customers
as she wrapped them.

How strange that she has
in abundance what she misses.

CHILDREN KNOW

We adults always ask questions:
What do you do?
Where do you live?
What do you think?

It's an endless list.

But when you watch children,
they get involved;
they like watching and listening
and playing with each other.

Their heart is their intellect,
at least for now.

Wouldn't it be nice if it
stayed that way forever?

ANGELS

The little ones tell us
that they see them
and talk with them.

I am surprised, pleased,
and a bit envious.

I have a lot to ask the angels
but the little ones don't;

I guess that's why they don't
come:

My mind is always getting in
the way.

ELUSIVE BUTTERFLY OF LOVE

"He who binds himself to joy
does the winged life destroy,"
wrote Blake.

And after all these years
I try to do this every day.

But the bird escapes
no matter how hard I try

And flies away for another
to pursue.

And I am left with empty hands,
empty heart,

Knowing I will start all over again.

The heart has this same treasure.
Why didn't I start there
in the first place?

THE WISE ONES

The wise ones come and go
quietly.
They see and understand
and do good acts;
and they are gone.

Their words, acts, and wisdom
are recorded
in the great books

But seldom practiced by
the others:
the ones who have not
reached this state,
the ones who profess goodness
but do not live it.

What a paradox
is this grey land
between goodness
and action.

Everything seems to
die there.

The wise ones remind us:
"See the truth as goodness,
and put goodness
into action."

SILENCE

I can hear the train in the distance;
the sound gradually fades
and there is silence.

Now the dogs bark some distance
away: It sounds as if
they're chasing something.

And the dawn is cool and
fresh and
there is silence again.

Now the birds talk
to each other:
they will do this all day.

And we will do the same
until it is time for night
and silence again,

When we can go inside for a while
to a place where all noises
begin and end.

WILD TURKEY

I went walking this morning
before dawn.

As I walked up a hill
I came upon a turkey farm.
All the birds were gobbling away
inside the pen

But one had
escaped.

He was outside, free at last
to escape the hatchet.

And what was he doing
but pacing the wire net,
seeking a way back inside
to his family.

Some things matter more
than survival.

TWILIGHT

As I draw closer to leaving
I ask myself,

Do I have everything I'll need
for the journey?

Have I done all the things I should?

Usually, it's only a few weeks –
whatever I've forgotten
can be done later.

But I'm reminded on this trip
there is no returning.

I have to finish everything here
and take only the essentials.

There is no room for maya.
The food that will nourish me
are the qualities.

Have I got them all? It's
getting late, best try and gather
a few more before
nightfall.

You never know.

WISE CHILD

The Pennsylvania Dutch have a saying:
"We get too old too soon, too wise
too late."

I knew a little girl once but
she was different.

She was wise already: curious
about life and she
loved ice cream.

But the true sweetness she savored
was in the hearts of others
and her own.

And this quiet force
carried her through life until

She died at thirteen.

THE BEAST

Try as I may
I can't get away

From this thing.

From whence is its
power?

It is interminable.

It haunts me,
not from in front
but from behind
somewhere inside,
invisible,

Just waiting to pounce
or slither in …

And once established
refuses to leave

And spoils all the
fruits and vegetables.

Oh, that I could
dispense with it swiftly
at a single blow.

But the nature of the beast requires
a constant effort to kill,

And just when you think
it's safe to relax, it rears
its ugly head –
better than a cat with nine lives,
this one has a thousand.

Will I ever see its end? This I?

PATIENCE

Conscience is easy;
acting on it is very difficult.

I can only draw from
the other side,

The side from whence comes
all life good and bad.

God understands – that's
why He gave us patience.

Please flood my heart and soul
with this quality:

It is my only hope
in this daily struggle.

THOUGHTS ON THE CRUISE SHIP

We met Mr. Oshima and his wife
after dinner.

I took their photo
and spoke my few words of Japanese.

At first, he was formal in his manner
and stiff.

Yet, when I told him how lovely
his people were

He smiled and instantly I saw
in that smile

The face that removes barriers between nations
and between people.

THE REVOLUTION

The moment of revolution came peacefully
as in a dream.

The old power so strong,
so decadent, so evil

Refused to concede,
to go peacefully.

But the new order came,
a force sweeping through the countryside;

Even those who had not seen it
were moved by it.

And surrender came throughout the land:
peaceful, gracious – at times, begrudgingly.

But it was in each heart
that the moment of truth had come,

And with it a new order:
goodness, compassion, and duty.

What a wonder.

THE INVISIBLE ONE

We carry with us
the invisible passenger.

He sits quietly observing,
calm and serene

While all around us is
motion, haste, mind, and desire.

We change our clothes,
our expressions, our thoughts,
our words, our actions.

And the invisible passenger
never changes – He stays the same.

Sometimes, I become the
invisible one, quiet, serene,
and peaceful.

Though it usually lasts only a brief time.

And I am back again with
my judgments and deadlines.

What am I to do?
These two parts of me
seem at odds but still
live together.

When I asked the Sage he told me,
"This is the true jihad, the true
inner struggle."

A STRANGE FELLOW, THIS MIND

What a strange fellow
this mind is.

He knows that at
my center

Lies the treasure of the ages.

He knows that entering
this inner sanctum

Provides instantly the peace
that surpasseth all understanding.

Yes, the mind is a
strange fellow.

For he woos us into the forest
day in and day out,

Convincing us of his sincerity
and illusory good.

And we listen and obey.

Only when we present
the treasure face to face
does he shrink back and hide.

What a strange fellow
this mind is.

FOLLIES

Watching the Follies
I thought of the old days

And heaved a sigh.

Not bad all these legs
and breasts, I thought to
myself.

Am I missing something?
the little voice inside asked.

You could go back
and this time
really enjoy the games.

God gives us these wonders
of the flesh

As a lesson:
It's really Desires 101:

Once you pass it you
understand and move

To the graduate program.

The alphabet is fine
for a child,

But now it's time to read.

CRUISE STOP

We've arrived at Trieste;
it's really the Best!

Say the books on this region,
the stories are legion.

Time to get off
and wander about.

Fettucina, pasta, sauerkraut,
Café Express: heavenly mess.

A dream to be here
but at night by the pier

Lies our glorious ship.
What a pip.

No need to explore,
just open the door.

All halls lead to Rome,
our home away
from home.

EYES

Eyes are the mirrors of
the soul, it is said.

And each day, for a
split second, I see in

A stranger that
quick recognition

That fades even before
it is understood.

Would that we could
prolong it

Just until we have
understood

That precious unity that
joins us all.

SMILES

A hundred smiling faces
every morning.

They could be frowning
or even blank

But instead each day
they are smiling.

Isn't it a wonder
what a smile will do
to a room.

It's as if a bright warm
light were turned on.

Everyone benefits from it
and all the shadows
disappear.

It is said, by your children
shall ye be taught.

And here we have inside us
these childrens' smiles:

Coming from adults,
reminding us of
the choices we make
each moment.

A SUMMER CRUISE

Only twelve days on a ship,

Making its way through
foreign waters

Yet nurturing in its own space

A security, freedom, and
awareness

That we often lack
at home.

Knowledge that this
short time is precious.

Could we not carry
it home and

Keep it beside us
from sunup to sundown?

This inward cruise is
indeed the most precious.

LEAVING

Leaving after twelve days
on board is sad.

I didn't know any of
these people before

And now some are like
family.

Have I missed something?

I meet new people each day
at home but I feel
no sadness leaving them.

Travel reminds us of our
journey.

All these different people,
all going to the
same place.

Maybe that's what
makes it so precious.

THE CAMPO

Shouting, talking, sitting, and watching
in the Campo.

All were aware of the full moon rising near the tower

But only a few watched it,
the others content to walk in its light.

The scene was bathed in moonlight,
a sense of coolness and calm.

It was as if the hurry of life
had slowed to
a walk

And finally they could
savor why they were here.

This dessert of the day's meal
was sweet and nourishing,
its flavor
tasted by all.

Such a rare moment.

SIENA

We walked on the Campo
last night

where families and couples
strolled under a rising moon.

There was a strange stillness
yet quiet exuberance
among those gathered on this
fall evening.

It was unlike anything
I had seen for a long while.

In many cities
when more than a few gather
there is noise,
and energy which seems ready
to burst forth.

Here all was calm – even
the pace at which people strolled.

No one was in a hurry,
it seemed. Why go
somewhere else?

Is this a normal evening in Siena?
To me it is
quite rare.

THE PIAZZA

It was a warm fall night
on the piazza.

Silver grey clouds
floated past a rising moon.

Scattered around the campo were couples talking,

Men playing with their children,

Families strolling together
and friends laughing:

Everything to write home about.

Even with thousands of people
there was no shouting
or drunks or beggars.

There was a calm
that hovered lightly around the piazza.

There seemed no ulterior motives,

Only enjoying and accepting
the wonder of our existence.

HOME AWAY FROM HOME

A new home:
a resting place,
a place of quiet.

Why do we
need this so much
when we have it
already inside?

My father whispers,
Be patient,
wait and watch
as the flower unfolds.

I can smell the fragrance
already, but clouds of
doubt and confusion
obscure the path.

Time for a cup of tea.
He said,
Be aware, that is all.
Be grateful for your
blessings and
do your duties.

The rest will come
as God wills It..

BARKING DOGS

All night they go at it –
yap, yap, yap
gr-ow, ow, ow.
Hardly time to rest.

Inside listening –
we wonder, why is there
so much noise? Why
do our pets annoy us so?

But then – I understand
the barking dog is inside,
always entering my peace
and telling me: get up --
look around – scratch your itch.

Wouldn't it be nice to
turn down the volume,
or even better – turn it off?

Easier said than done, say I.
But the Sage smiles
and hands me a gift.

Just use this, he says;
it will give you peace.

It's a small book but
the title is obscured.
I think it says Surrender –
but to be sure I must open it
and start reading.

WINDING WAY

The road curves
gently through the
hills and forests.

It is quite lovely
and peaceful –
each turn bringing a
new vista.

No hurry –
not even sure
of the time
or turns.

But we know
the direction is right, and
we arrive home.

That is all
that
really matters.

BLACKBERRY BUSH

I drove past it
many times.

I walked past it
twice
never noticing
the berries.

There they were –
shining black,
juicy and asking
to be picked.

My hands could carry
only so much.

I'll stop tomorrow
with a bigger bag.

Why doesn't everyone
see these and take them,
I thought.

"You have to be aware,"
the Sage told me
smiling.

Our treasures lie
right before us --
under our nose.
We need only pick and
taste.

WHAT A LOVELY ROOM

What a lovely room
this is.

So large and tall and
stately and quiet.

Holding many secrets
but only suggesting

What it must have
seen over the centuries.

And here am I
sitting in time wondering:

Can I take this moment
and coax from it wisdom
and understanding?

The room will then
have done its duty
and I, mine.

What a wonder:
this room, this life.

HOW DO WE PROCEED?

Show me, oh God
how to use Your grace.

How to control the mind.
How to find peace
in each moment.

I know it is possible
for You to bring
tears of understanding
to my eyes and heart,

And in these moments
my faith is reborn
and all things are one.

Can you make this
your steady state?
asks the voice inside.

But God, in His wisdom,
only smiles and
His grace flows
in its own way and time.

We need only surrender.

TAMING THE BEAST

Taming the Beast is
difficult

But sometimes it happens
without effort

And the mind is
quiet and for a second.

I can sense and know
what is possible;

Then the clouds fill up the opening

And it is grey again
and joyless.

Finding fault, judging,
backbiting – arrogance:

These clouds can all
be dispersed by the sun.

That light is so peaceful
it need only be, and

We receive the rays
gratefully.

There is no effort involved.
Why then do I struggle?

The Sage smiles. "Let go," he says,
"and look only at the good."

And this is the Jihad.

ANOTHER QUIET DAY

Before, I used to swim
in the morning
and lie in the sun.

All too pleasant,
and why not?
This is vacation.

But now, after prayers
I read slowly and carefully
the words of my father.

So little time, yet
all the time
in the world.

The Sage tells us
not to hurry, but reminds us
of the value of each
minute.

Used correctly
we climb the ladder;
ignored we fall back.

You can't make a
flower bloom by
forcing it.

In time, with food
and care, it will
bring forth a most
beautiful blossom.

WE GOT LOST

What a nice journey
along a ridge line,

Looking into verdant
valleys below.

On the way home
we explored a little,

leaving the ridge line
to move in the valley.

Here there are many roads – but
no view of where they lead.

We took a few and
found ourselves lost.

The clear view from the ridge was gone

And we were caught up
in the twists and turns
of the roads.

Not a sign to tell us
our whereabouts.

With only the sun as our guide
we moved East
to find the road home.

THE MUSEUM

Archaeology – the study
of people and things past.

Such a nice clean
organized place, this museum.

Each room showing a
period in man's progress.

Making fire, making pots,
making knives.

All this has brought us to modern life.

The scholars speak of
progress; yet TODAY
bombs kill more in a minute
than a century of fighting
in the past.

The original man
was not primitive.

He spoke with God
and walked in grace.

The museum collects
vestiges of another world.

THE POINT

She – He -- It
What is the It?
We know the she and he.

IT speaks of the omnipresent,
That which is always
and always will be
and always was.

The Truth is so much
before us, in us,
and around us that we
have become forgetful of it.

Lacking the will, the faith,
the wisdom to
acknowledge it
and more important, to
understand it,

We continue on our paths
hoping each turn
will give us the reward –
the peace that all life suggests
and then denies.

With each other
we sometimes argue
sometimes fight
sometimes embrace.

But that which comforts us
and draws us together
is the inherent realization
that the point in each of us
is the same and eternal.

AT THE WINDOW

What shall I write this
clear morning as I
sit by the window?

I see etched on the near
hillside, five trees against
the sky.

Dark, quiet forms that
reassure my
existence and awareness.

Over the hill – I know not
what to expect.
"Surely goodness and mercy
will follow me all the
days of my life."

WHAT CAN WE DO?

One minute -- the world
is at our doorstep: a smile,
a touch – the warmth
of goodness –
what else is true?

The next – a cloud in
the sky, then more,
then wind, then a storm.
Words kindle even more
unrest.

And suddenly again, a
strong wind sweeps all away
and the sun is there in its
warmth and beauty.

But, I have known
cloudy days where my heart
is smiling and I
am at one with all.

Why is this state taken
from me? Do I give it
or is it stolen?
What can I do?

In the beginning, the small plant
is buffeted by the wind and rain;

But in time it grows
toward the sun and
becomes strong and glistens
even in the storm
and gives forth lovely fruits
and shade from the
summer sky.

GOING HOME

My heart is aching.
I know what it needs
I know how to get it.

But I sit – smitten
by a sense of malaise,
unwilling to cope.

Why does the salmon
keep swimming upstream
past all obstacles and even
the current?

It has a duty which
lies deep in its heart
to perform.

And we -- much wiser
and aware – cannot even
hurdle the first waterfall.

Oh my, what a
desperate state –
second even to a fish.

The Sage comforts us
and says, "Move towards
the light – the shadows will
fall behind."

CLEANING THE SPOT

He said the white cow has
a single black spot and
that is where we look.

The cow is almost all white
but not quite good enough for
white-cow heaven.

And, as for us, what
do we do with our
spots?

We can't trade in our
skin. NO – he meant
the black spot inside.

The spot of arrogance.
This can be removed by
constant scrubbing.

Patience, tolerance, forgiveness,
understanding are the
scouring agents.
They do their job well
et
Voila –
A WHITE COW.

But remember, this may
take years of scrubbing.
Are you ready?

Part Two

THE FLOWER

Isn't it strange
that we talk so much
about goodness?

If we have the right
vision, we can see it
all around us in
the eyes of others.

Even as they
hurry past us
on the street.

Yet often it remains
hidden, only a glimmer
in the dark of
work and worry.

If we part the branches
of the rose bush
we can see the flower
and smell its fragrance.

How do we
open the hearts
of those around us?

Good morning, neighbor!

TERRITORY

Dogs mark their territory:
They leave their stain
on the ground to keep
others out.

Our territory is more
subtle: it involves
doing things our way and
having our opinions.

Yet we mark it
clearly all the same,
just like the dog.

If one is to enter
he must do so
at his own risk.

Is there a land where
there are no boundaries?

The quiet voice within
speaks of the true heart:
Anyone can enter;
only pride is kept out.

SHARKS

Recently I read of people
being killed by
sharks while swimming in
the ocean.

Should we stop
swimming? What are
we to do?

There are worse things
than sharks: There are
the animals that swim
just beneath the surface
of our mind.

If we're not careful
they will wound or
even kill us.

Everything we do
should be done with
thought and compassion.

If we act without thought
we open the door
to the sharks

And sure enough they
will come.
We have to swim
carefully in
this life.

EXPEDIENCY

It is said the Prophet harmed
no living thing.

The other day I saw a
cockroach and crushed it.

Then I felt
guilty.

I'm certainly not the
Prophet, said I.

God sends His chosen
to teach us.

By example they
instruct.

The rest is up to us.

In Japan I used to
catch insects
and set them free
outside.

But
I have changed.
It's too much
trouble now.

God, you must
come and awaken
the compassion within.

HABITS

We learn to eat, to talk,
to act, to discriminate,
even to kill.

We learn many habits
and they all come
after the original one.

As infants, there is
only one habit –
the purity and peace
of God within.

We can see it in
the eyes of a child. It is
a wonder.

As time passes, we
learn the other habits
and forget the
original one.

If we nourished the
original state we
would have no need
for the others.

All action would
flow perfectly from
the center.

THE BEHOLDER

Beauty is in the eye
of the beholder.
So is ugliness.

So easy for us to see
ugliness in others –
it makes us
feel better

Because we are not
so ugly.

Yet if we were
really beautiful
inside, everyone we
saw would be
beautiful.

The mother sees her
child born with
one arm as
a gift from God.

True joy, true unity,
true compassion see no
faults.

How do we erase these
inner faults?

The Sage says it takes only
the brush of determination
and the soap of wisdom.
But we have to scrub hard.

THE COMPASS

If we set our compass to
the right azimuth we
will arrive at our
destination.

But if we change even
by one degree our
original setting, we
will not arrive home.

The path is like this:
A white wall washed clean
will show clearly
a single spot.

If our intention is to
remain clean, we
must always find that
spot and clean it.

This is our task each
day: make no mistake –
there is always a
spot, or two.

God gave us the best
solvents: intention
and effort.
The Sage tells us
this is all we need.

What are we
waiting for?

THE SNOW GOOSE

When I lived abroad I
had a favorite poem I
would recite for
anyone.

"The Snow Goose need not
bathe to make itself white;
neither need you do aught
but be yourself."

"How wonderful," I thought,
"and how easy." I lived
this way for years.

One morning as I thought
of the Snow Goose I
had a revelation:

The Snow Goose is
really busy all the time
cleaning itself.

Oh dear, what have I
been doing all these years?
I've been bathing
each day but I'm
still dirty.

Time to start cleaning
and stop reciting
poetry, said the
wise one within.
There's still time.

THE FIG TREE

There's a fig tree near
my house.

I walked by it many times
without seeing the fruit.

One day I noticed and
started to pick.

The tree was on a steep
hill and the work was hard.

But I continued and carried
these fruits home.
They were so good!

It is like this in our
life.

The fruit tree of qualities
is right
under our nose;
yet we often walk by
without seeing
the fruits.

Picking is difficult but
the fruits are
delicious.

Patience, compassion
and wisdom have a
special sweetness.

LEARNING

When I was a child
I learned to spell;

I could not imagine
reading.

Here we are as adults
living day to day;

We cannot imagine
the next stage.

The child thinks forming
a letter is success;

We think living a day
is success.

If we only knew
what lies ahead,
what is possible;

But for this we
need a special
kind of teacher.

THE FLASHLIGHT

When we push the switch
the light emerges;

When we push again
it disappears.

It is like this
with our lives.

The Sage tells us the
soul belongs to God;

When He pushes
the switch it
returns to Him.

All that is left
is the bulb & battery.

We should hurry
before the battery
wears out.

STUDENTS

Perhaps we are
going the wrong way.

At one point the
child wishes to
discard his toys and

Become a man.

But all the wise ones
tell us we must
become again
as little children.

We strive to be
teachers – but
what can we teach?

If we become true
students we will
pass the teacher.

There is only one
teacher.

His lesson for the day
is surrender.

THE SEED

The seed within at first
is tiny.

It is the seed of
goodness.

If we nurture it, it grows and
something wondrous
happens.

The seed takes over
our being and
we die in it.

If we die before
we die

Then we never die,
said the Sage.

But this process
of our death

Requires absolute
Faith.

And then the
miracle happens.

THE MOVIE

The mind is our
movie house.

We enter it
and are
entranced.

We live the lives
and passions
on the screen,

And when it
is finished
the lights go on.

All that is
left is the
screen;

The rest was
illusion.

For a brief time
we believed.

This is the mind.
And we must
leave it

And go outside
into the world.

But this is also
illusion, the
Sage tells us.

The true
reality lies inside
where the
screen receives
only the
purest light.

HERO FISH

The fish lives in
the ocean
where the water
is salty.

It can never find
pure water there.

If it is to change
it must leave
its home

But only a brave
fish would do this –
one in a million.

If we were to leave
our mind and enter
the heart

We would find the
pure essence

And know the reason
for our creation.

But only one in
a million would
do this.

WHAT IS THE USE?

What is the use of
talking?

What is the use of
complaining?

What is the use
of hoping?

If we have eyes
to see

Then we can
see beyond all
this.

The answer lies
within

But does not
give itself
readily.

We need faith
and certitude

To polish the
rough stone,

And then we
become the diamond.

A LIGHT

It is said one has a
choice in the darkness.

Either curse it or
light a light.

I cursed it for
a long time
but found it stayed there.

And then I
saw a light

That came from
a wise man.

Now when it
gets dark

I turn on
the light.
So much better

And besides I can
see to work.

THE SURGEON

Are we to operate
on the patient?

If we succeed he
lives and we
are praised.

If we fail he dies
and we are blamed.

But the true
surgeon is elsewhere.

Only He knows
the outcome and
will provide.

We are only
the instrument.

We only do the
operation. The
outcome is in
the hands of the
Master Surgeon.

We have finished
school – it's
time to operate.

DIFFICULTY

I used to avoid
difficulty at any cost.

I still do sometimes

But something has
happened.

The wise man
told me:

Every difficulty is a
lesson, a gift.

Inside the difficulty
lies the gem of wisdom.

We need patience to
endure

And then the dawn
comes.

Where there was
dark there is light

And we can see
the path ahead
clearly.

ESSENCE

What is the essence
of our being?

What is the power
that gives us life?

What is the grace
that protects us?

How can we
touch that which
already is?

What path is there
to reach
that point,

So we can bathe in that
bliss and
thank God for
this treasure?

There is only
this tiny point.

Make no mistake:

It is there for those
of us who die before
we die.

THE PRISM

All colors come
from the prism

But the prism is
without color.

What a wonder;
what a mystery.

If we were to
enter the prism

It would be
quiet and pure;

The mind would
be absent.

So where is the
key, asks the student.

The teacher tells us
we have to fashion it

Out of God's qualities;
only then will it
fit the lock.

STAINS

Some people wear
black.
Some wear white.

The Sage tells us
black requires
no washing;

We can't see
the dirt.

I like white
myself,

But it takes
a lot of washing
to keep it clean.

Why do I still
have fear –
where is my
faith?

Scrub, says the
Sage.

You must scrub
as if your life
depended on it.

And then the
stains will
disappear.

DUTY

Each animal has its duty:
The cow gives milk to
those in need,

The beaver builds dams
to make ponds,

The horse pulls the
cart for the farmer.

And man, what
are his duties?

Wife, family, children, and
business.

Is this what I have
come to do?

Even the apple tree
does service.

Can we serve as well
and quietly,
'
Never asking for
praise?

The acorn contains
the oak.

What is our seed
inside – what does
it contain?

When we
know this
we will know
our duty.

BELIEF

How can we believe in
what we don't see?

How can we pray to a
God we do not know?

Yet, God has given us
wisdom. It surrounds us.

A baby comes into this
world, innocent and fragile.

He is held, coddled and
fed. He lacks nothing.

Each thing we see is
a lesson.

We are as the baby
yet we have no trust.

The baby opens his
mouth and is fed.

We need a different
kind of food.

If we understand it,
one drop will suffice.

All our worries and
needs will be gone.

WHO AM I?

Nothing is coming to
my mind.

Of what can I write?
It has all been said.

Then what am I to do
with this time?

If I sit quietly and
watch the mind

I am struck by its
nature.
It never stops.

Even when I think it
is quiet

It is moving in many
directions under
the surface.

At the bottom of
the ocean there is
life.

All this is useless
unless we understand.

Even the animals know
instinctively.

They pray before they
sleep.

And we, who
have been given all,
use only a portion.

What is it
that asks the
question,
Who am I?

DOGS

Why does a dog trust
his master?

Even when treated
poorly he waits at
the door.

Even when punished
he returns to lick
the hand.

He would die for
his master,

He has such love and
faith.

Have we the
same with our
Father?

That which gave
birth to us is
invisible.

It only asks we
have faith and
remember.

Is this too much
to ask?

NOAH

Noah worked for
a long time on
his boat.

Everyone laughed.

But when
the floods came
everyone cried

Except Noah.

It is like this:

Even though we
see our family and
friends go
before us

We stand speechless,
afraid and ignorant.

Something inside
says – build the boat;

But we are too
intent on watching
the flood.

NESTS

If a bird's nest is
destroyed,
the mother immediately
starts another;
She feels no blame.

A Tibetan Sage built
a house seven times.
Each time his master
told him to
destroy it.

The last time he
started to rebuild
he felt no blame
or anger,

Just his duty in
building the house.
This time his master
didn't tell him to
destroy it.

Why then are we
so full of
these feelings?

If a bird
can show
flawless
duty,

Why do we get
so upset when
our car
won't start?

CLOWNS

It is said, clowns
are very serious.

Why do
I laugh, then?

They don't show
their sadness.

Accidents are
always happening to
clowns

And the more they
try, the more
they fail.

If only the clown
would wait a
few minutes

Everything would be
OK.

But we would have
nothing to laugh at

And the clown would
have no job.

Is this
the circus we live in?

EFFORT

Why is it every time I
try to meditate
or write I fall
asleep?

What is it that
hinders my
progress?

Surely
these good efforts
should be
helped.

Lest we forget,
there are two
sides to everyone

Just as there is
light and dark,
strong and weak.

That which holds
me back doesn't
like my effort.

It knows if I
try, it
will lose.

Duty is greater than
God, said the Sage.
How true.

TEACHER

Those with wisdom hear
the truth and weep.

Those ignorant of truth
listen to their mind.

We learn the alphabet
so we can read.

The teacher knows this;
as children we follow.

Now we are grown
and it's time to teach –

But what have we
learned to teach our
children?

All we give them
is wisdom
of the world;

They give us wisdom
of God.

Who then is teaching?
We need a teacher,

Only this one is
inside our very
heart.

DESTRUCTION

Yesterday the buildings
came down.

There was violence
and death.

Our orderly world
collapsed.

We were shocked,
then sad, then angry.

The salmon sees
many of its family
die on the way upstream.

It does not stop
to mourn but continues
its journey.

It has the strongest
need to fulfill its duty
before death.

What about us:
Do we strive towards
truth before we die?
Do we die before death?

SEED

Water is everywhere:
In our body, in the
air, in the ground,
in the sea.

Without it we can
not live. It
makes our life possible.

They have found
seeds thousands
of years old in
the pyramids.

When they
added water the
seeds came
to life.

The seed of our
body has grown
to full size.

What about the
seed of our soul:
Has it flowered?

There is a special water
it needs to
grow.

To serve
others we
need a
melting
heart.

HEART

The wise man tells us
at one instant man can
be a saint, in the next
a devil.

And that we must
never judge a person
on his bad actions.

Only God knows
the inner heart,
so there is hope
for us all.

If I could only
find the prankster
who replaces good fruit
with bad.

But if everything
is inside, then
it must be me
who is doing this.

If I keep my basket
covered, then
I will keep only
the good fruit.

Why is this so difficult?

DYING

What does it mean
to die before we
die?

Is it the body
we are speaking of
or something else?

The atom inside
which is our true life
is eternal.

All the prophets
and wise ones have
told us this.

We need only to
remove those
things which
block its light.

But,
arrogance,
envy, lust,
and anger don't
want to die.

Oh, is this
what it means
to die before
death?

WHAT IS IT?

It is so tantalizingly
close, this
mystery.

I can feel it
inside; it is
in my mind and
my heart.

I can feel it in
the air.
Death brings it
even closer.

Birth sings its
praises – it is
everywhere.

And I know if
I can only
touch it I
will be saved.

What a puzzle.
It already touches
me, but I can't
touch it.

Maybe if I let go
of my desire
it will take
me in.

THE VEIL

Have you ever been
to an aquarium?

It's truly a wonder
watching all
God's creatures swim by.

Only a thin glass
separates us from
their world.

It had better be
strong. I don't
want to drown.

And I'm sure
they wouldn't want
this world.

What is that veil
which separates us
from the truth?

It is very thin and
also very strong.
We can see
through it.

But we think
we must not
touch it.

The Sage tells us it's
an illusion. "If we trust
and reach out
we may have
the prize."

HEAVEN AND HELL

Finally, the Prophet allowed
his people to wage war.

It was after much
suffering and despair

at the hands of those
who raped and murdered.

But, the Prophet decreed
the rules of war were strict.

One could never hurt
innocent women or children.

If the opponent's sword fell
you had to pick it up and return it,

And the fight should
continue on an equal basis.

What then of someone
who professes Islam

And commits a
crime on helpless ones?

He believes he will
go straight to heaven.

The Sage tells us the
doors of hell are open for him.

MARRIAGE

The tiny acorn contains
the huge oak,

A tree that brings
shade to the weary

And provides us with
many gifts.

True marriage is
like the acorn:

If watered and cared for
it will prosper

And the rewards
will be many

As it rises towards
heaven.

If we become impatient
and discard it to start another

The seed will die
and we will not reap
our rewards.

It is the same with
marriage:

Much watering, much
work, much growth.

NOT SO LONG AGO

Not so long ago
children played in
the fields,

Neighbors greeted each
other with love,

Couples strolled in
the evening hand in hand.

How very sweet and
natural it was.

Now, the world
is in a great hurry.

Time is of the essence,
not to enjoy but to use.

Those who strolled
now trot;

Those who trotted
now run.

What have we come
here for?

Our father tells us
every day:
Have a melting heart
and serve others with this heart.

I can't do this while I'm running.

THINGS OF VALUE

So often things of value
are hidden,

Like the rose nestled
in the thorns

Or the gem hidden
in the rock

Or the pearl within
the oyster.

Yet there are those
who shout their wares

Extolling the excellence
of their product.

It looks good but
something is wrong.

Things of value
whisper – they
never shout.

And so it is with
a man of wisdom.

They come so rarely
that we must

Hold on for dear life
when we find one.

MY CAT

I have a cat that
comes by my house.

I chase him away
because he eats the birds.

My neighbor next door
feeds his cat;

Then he has no hunger
for birds.

Why didn't I think
of this?

Well, I did, but
it takes so much work.

Much easier to
shout, "Go away!"

My hungry cat continues
to eat birds.

I watch my neighbor's cat
come to be scratched.

It is a lovely sight,
such trust from a
wild animal.

Can we do this
with each other?

MOVIES

We don't want to leave
the movie house.

Our hearts and minds
filled with
sounds and colors.

But when it is over we
file outside into the sunlit world,

From one movie house to another.
But the outside world
is not as pleasant
as the movie.

It demands an involvement:
We must eat, work,
suffer and die.

It's much nicer inside
the movie house – dark
and quiet.

Let's go back inside – we
can stay for a while.

Some of us spend our lives like
this – escaping duties
and drawing the
bedsheet back
over our heads.

I never saw a bee sleep.
He has no movie house.
What wonderful honey
he makes.

STORM

It's difficult in a
snowstorm to trace our
steps back.

As soon as they are made
the points are covered by
snow and wind.

What was so clear
becomes invisible in
a short time.

But we have a goal, no
need to return – that way
holds only danger.

Ahead we can see
dimly in the distance
a light.

There is a cabin warm and safe
inside, against the
storm.

No time to stop – we
must continue; it
seems forever.

When we arrive it's
already daylight and
the storm has gone.

Let us enter in:
the host awaits
us with food
and drink

HOW?

It is hard to accept
that we cannot do
this work.

After all we have a
body, mind,
heart and soul.

Yet the exquisite tasks
we need performed
Only God can do.

Whenever we try to
fight this battle we
gain a bit and lose.

There never seems
to be that sure
progress

That marks Success.

How do I admit
I cannot do it
myself?

How do I surrender
to that powerful
grace – that completes?

This is the quandary
of my life and my
true yearning.

WE MUST NOT STOP

It is so easy to begin
a task – even to stay
with it a while.

But a lot of us never
finish it. Only a
few stay the course.

It seems there's
something inside
that gives us permission
to stop.

The other voice within
that tells us to
continue needs
reminding.

It's not that the
procrastinator is evil;
it's just his job.

We have the choice
and once we understand
that power

The work becomes
easier – the road
slopes downhill.

SIRENS IN THE NIGHT

They come unannounced,
rising in an eerie
crescendo and dropping
off to begin again.

Why is the sound so
impelling, so disturbing?
It's almost telling us
something.

So we sit and listen and
our mind jumps
from thought to
feeling, back and forth.

Finally
the sound subsides
and we are at peace
again for a while.

Sirens are needed to
alert us that something
important is happening.

Whenever we hear them
we listen more intently;
our whole being awakens.

There's another siren inside –
quieter, subtle, insistent.
It reminds us of the work
to be done.

INTERPRETER

I knew a lady once
in Paris;

She spoke no French
but understood people.

I watched her once
listen to a French man
who spoke no English.

When he finished she
told him
what he had said.

He was amazed as was
I.

I asked, how do you
do that?

She said, you have to
listen to the
heart.

I believe her. Children
can do the same thing.

This is a gift we
all have but most have
forgotten.

We need to
remember this and start
using it again

So we can listen to
those around us who
need our hearts.

HOME

I once heard a story of a dog
that was taken to a
place hundreds of miles
from its home.

It somehow found
its way back to the
very house it lived in.

No compass, no map,
no guide. How amazing.

In my journey
I seem to be coming
closer to my home.

It's still
quite a ways.

Do you think I'll
make it before
winter?

I certainly hope so.

HONEY

The most popular
girl in my school

Was the one who
never kissed a boy.

All the other girls
were popular

But
she drew boys like a
flower draws bees.

Everyone smelled the
fragrance and sweetness.

She was a gentle
girl, more kind than
beautiful.

It seems we all
needed that
special taste of
long ago.

PURE COLOR

Green is my favorite
color:
the color of nature
the color of growth
the color of health.

They say it is the
chlorophyll that makes
things green.

Chlorophyll has so
many purposes:
cleaning
purifying
nourishing.

What is the color
of the wise man,

What gives him a
special fragrance?

I once smelled ambrosia, musk
and sandalwood
while I sat near him.

It was heavenly; I
remember it well.

But he never wore
perfume, I knew.
Then where did that
fragrance come from?

TAPROOT

When you point your
finger at someone

The other three point back
towards you.

We never think of this
in our judgments.

The kind man
doesn't judge others;

He tries to understand
and help.

All the energy that
could go into blame
goes into love.

Kindness is our true
nature, the taproot
of our life

From which comes
the shade, flowers,
and fruit of the tree.

HARVEST

Fall is my favorite time.
Everything has come full circle.

Leaves are golden red:
the harvest is in

And the heavy work
is done.

We have time to
savor the fruits of
our labor.

The next season
brings cold and hardness
to the earth.

Then the farmer
repairs his tools and
plans for the next year.

What of us – what
plans do we have
for tomorrow?

I have come to see
all days as the same,
all seasons as the same.

There is only
one crop I need
to attend to: its
fruit lasts forever.

SLEEP

I welcome this
guest each night.

He is usually a friend
but I never know
what he'll bring me.

I do know that he is
temporary and that morning
will bring the dawn.

They say this is the
little sleep and that
death is the big one.

What kind of dawn
can I expect, if any?

Will there be nightmares
or pleasant dreams?

Sleep restores, quiets and
prepares us for the
work to be done.

For the big sleep
the work must be
done already.

ZIKR

When we were
children and upset

We would run to
our mother

And she would take us
in her arms,

Rocking and soothing us
till we were peaceful again.

We can't do this
anymore – but we
need peace.

Within each breath is
a power that
cleans us, soothes us
and brings us back
to our true parent.

Once we learn
this power
we have found the
source of our life.

We then become
the parent
who receives the child
and restores him to
his true state.

JAPANESE BEETLES

These beetles destroy
my beautiful roses
each year.

They come in droves and
eat everything good.
It is a sight.

No matter how much
I spray, they prosper
and do their damage.

There is a microbe
tiny and powerful. If
you water the ground
with it in the Fall

It will go in the
earth and eat the
beetle larvae.

Why didn't I think
of this before?

I've got another
kind of beetle
even more persistent:

It eats my good qualities
and destroys
everything good.

But now I have a
microbe that kills it.
I can't forget to water
each day.

LIONS

Did you ever watch
lions?

They often fight
with each other
over food.

But this is their
nature.

When they have
eaten they lie
down beside
one another
and lick away the
wounds.

When we fight
the wounds
won't heal.

They become scars,
painful to
touch.

We won't lie
down next to
the one who
caused them.

Instead we will
hunt him in
the night, catch
and kill him.

We have so
much to learn
from the animals.

PICTURES

Before, when we
took a picture we
had a true imprint
of our subject.

The color, form and
makeup of our
picture was true.

Sometimes we had
to wait hours or days
to capture this shot.

Now this has all
changed. There is no
true picture anymore.

Our machines can
make a picture seem
real. They borrow a
little from here and there.

The result is next to
perfect – no need to
wait and work to make
a good picture.

Hasn't something
been lost along
the way?

HEART AND MIND

Our mind is so fast
it travels the world
in a second.

It is always way
ahead of our
heart – peeking
around each corner.

Our heart is a
patient traveler.
He just plods on.

He doesn't have
the quickness of
mind nor the
cleverness.

But wherever he
walks there is
a beauty and
flowers grow.

It's hard to explain:
I would really like
to follow the mind;

But just see how
this wonder has
filled my life.

NET

Each fishing line might catch
one a fish for the village.

But if we took all the
lines and wove them
into a net

We could catch many
more, enough even to
dry for winter.

If we wove our good
qualities together to
form a net
of wisdom,

With this net
we could collect God's grace,
enough to nourish
us forever.

We have to be
the one to make
this net and
cast it in the
right place.

Then our work is done.

BURDENS

We have so many
heavy burdens.

We cannot drop a
single one.

Our life is so full
of anxiety and sorrow;

These things we
carry are useless.

The Sage tells us to
drop them

And replace them
with wisdom.

It is very light
and has great
clarity.

If we are able to
do this we will
see,

And never again
will we travel
with burdens.

THE BOAT

This world we travel in
is like the ocean:

There are millions of
creatures below.

Some are very dangerous;
they would kill us.

We need a boat to
travel the surface
and reach our goal.

This boat is made of
the planks of
good qualities.

It is only when we stop
using them

That we develop leaks
and gradually sink

beneath the surface.

We need to watch
carefully for any
holes and repair
them quickly
with the glue of wisdom.

HABITS

You know how it
is with habits:

You have to do
something one
hundred times

To get it right.

Why is this so
difficult?

Shouldn't once be
enough?

But we forget that
we have two sides.

One wants to
finish; the other
wants to delay.

If we say I'll do
it tomorrow – then
we never do it.

The Now requires effort;
Light has to tell
dark to go away.

This is the connection
between wisdom and body.

Body is here to do the
work of wisdom.

ADAM

There is a strange
space between our
wishes and
our actions.

What is this area
in which even
the best intentions
disappear?

We certainly
know
what is best
for us.

We know the path to
grace.

But we keep forgetting
that God allowed
Iblis to disobey.
We have the same right.

Adam saw the light
and asked forgiveness.
He had to start
all over again to gain
what he once had.

And with us it is the
same each day of
our lives.

LSD

I once took LSD –
everyone said it
would change my life.

Well, it did, sort of.
I saw things I
had only imagined.

I experienced fears and
joys I could only have
dreamed of.

And when it was
done I woke up
and found myself
back where I
had started.

In the world of the
mind there are so many
wonders. They mesmerize;
they are almost real.

But if we look with
wisdom we see they are
only pictures.

To be nourished we
need food, not pictures.

There is a special kind
of food we need
to complete our task.
It comes from the heart.

MY WALK

Every morning I go
for a walk.

Sometimes I don't
want to; it is chilly
outside.

But then again I
know the benefits
and open the door.

It is cold and I
walk fast to stay
warm.

Then I begin to
feel better; the rhythm
of my legs is
strengthening.

Then I am warm and
glad I came.

I watched the Sage
try to speak when he was
ill.

He had a duty but
he was frail and
had little strength.

But he began and then
a strange thing
happened. What
should have drained him
strengthened him, and
at the end he was
vibrant.

This how
it is with
my walk and
also my life.

DOG

Did you ever
watch a dog
chase his
tail?

We laugh: silly
animal!

Doesn't it know
it's part of
itself?

The 18,000 universes
lie within.

Everything we
chase is
part of ourself.

Why don't we
stop? It's
useless.

The dog inside
knows no
better.

Something
inside watches
the dog and
tells it to
stop.

We should listen!

WHY?

Why would someone do this,

Kill thousands of innocents?

Were his family murdered
by a stranger,

Would he be tolerant?

Who is the enemy?

After we have sifted
all the facts we
are left with one:

The enemy is
inside.

The Jihad is in
ourselves.

The true enemy is
neither rich nor
poor.

The true enemy
lies in our mind
not our heart.

JIHAD

They speak of JIHAD,
these people.

Kill the enemy, they
say.

You can kill insects
by the thousands

Yet they keep coming
back.

It only takes one to
start it all over.

Our enemy lies in caves
we say – in the dark.

But even if we destroy
the caves

There is still darkness
in the world.

The darkness is our
ignorance.

This is the true
enemy.

It lies within each
of us.

It cannot be killed
by battle,

Only by wisdom.

SATAN

Make no mistake:
Satan is alive and well

In each of us.

He doesn't like the
light; he prefers the
darkness of ignorance.

We may kill
thousands in the
name of God

But this won't
touch the true
villain.

What are we to
do, then?

Of course we need to
keep our door
locked in the night;

There are always
robbers around.

But meanwhile, there
is much to do.

In the darkness we
have a choice – curse it
or light a light.

Satan hates
light. He
can't exist
in it.

To see the truth as
goodness and to put
this into action is
our only hope.

MY FRIEND

I have a friend who
is diabetic.

Each time I see him
he seems to have
lost a piece of his
body.

But he is always
happy, philosophic.

He tells me God
is simply taking him
piece by piece.

Not only is my
friend undiminished,
he seems helped
by his illness.

It hasn't touched his
essence.

That within us that
never dies is what
we need to cherish
in these times.

If we die before we
die then we never
die – says the Sage.

The wise ones mourn
only their lack of
Truth.

WHAT ARE WE TO DO

All around us is
chaos. Violence,
murder, destruction.

Is this God's world,
we ask.

God created both
good and evil, lest
we forget.

It is we who have
the choice.

Some choose evil
and we suffer
their acts.

They are the perpetrators,
not God.

What they receive
after this world is
unspeakable.

But we must not
embrace revenge
or the dark side;

Our only focus
should be on
our inherent goodness,
our path to God.

OUR CLASSROOM

It is said we
come from God

And to Him we
return.

What then is this
sojourn on Earth?

To fully know our
true nature,

We must see its
opposite.

This is the world:
It dies and is reborn.

Suffering abounds
wherever we look.

This is our
classroom – we have
come to learn.

There we take the
exam: pass or fail.

Have we learned
why we are here?

Do we understand
the peace that passeth
all understanding?

All this is but a whisper.
Our souls
are forever.

ANGER

Hastiness is the
father of anger.

Anger is the father
of evil.

We must be careful.

Big things start
with little things.

A virus for example,
or a tiny hole in
the dam.

It's not as hard
as it sounds.

Look before you leap.
Stop for a second
or two,
or three.

Then our old friend
wisdom will
come in

And we
can get on with
our lives in a better
way.

THE POSSE

We have been taught
that winning is everything.

In school, in business, in
sports, this is the only thing
that matters,

Because if we win we
are happy – at peace
with ourselves.

Isn't it odd that
the one contest
most important
is unseen.

In our westerns we
root for the
good guy.

Bad guys wear
black and slink around
in the shadows.

It is this way inside:
Good guys are everywhere
but silent.

All we see and hear are
the bad guys.

It is time the good
guys rode into
town.

ARTICHOKE

Did you ever eat an
artichoke? So
much work.

Many leaves to peel
away until we
reach the heart.

But oh, what a
delicious treat to
arrive there.

This is the story
of our lives.

At the center is
this beautiful
fruit – wonderful
to taste;

Yet so much peeling
needs to be done to
taste it.

We have nothing
but time – let's
start peeling.

THE WATER OF OUR SOUL

We need water to
live, to wash and to
drink.

The Soul also needs water.

The well we have
started is being
drilled.

The bit goes deeper
and deeper into the
earth.

But only dust so far.

It's so important
to keep digging.

The Sage tells us
it's down there.

We can see how
the earth is changing:

The soil is not dry
anymore

And now we see
moisture in the earth.

Don't stop now –
it's just around
the corner.

THE SQUIRREL

We have so much
to learn from animals.

Look at the squirrel:
Not one to complain.

Just busy finding
nuts and storing them.

His is serious work;
he knows winter is near.

Each step, each nut
is the difference between
Life and Death.

How're we doing
with our gathering?

Yesterday I found
a few

But today I have
to go to the city.

Tomorrow I may
be traveling.

I'll never manage
this way.

Winter is coming;
I'm way behind
schedule.

WHAT WORRY?

Our lives are so
full of worries.

Our children, our
bills, our jobs.

I watched the
wise man for a while.

He was deadly
serious in his work.

He had much to do
of great importance.

He had many people and
problems to deal with.

I never saw him
frown or worry;

Only a smile came
from his heart.

How could he be
so serene?

He told us not to
worry. He told us
where the smile is.

He gave us
the key to
this peace.
Where have we put it?

AGING

They say things get
better with time;

Great works of art,
perhaps people.

There's a fig tree
near my house.

I pick the ripe green
figs that are soft;

I leave the old
ones leathery and brown.

But yesterday I
took one anyway.

When I got home I
split open its tough skin

And inside was the
sweetest fruit of all.

Often the old ones,
the wise ones

Are the ones with
the sweetest fruit.

We should know
this as we go
about
our lives.

HURRYING

He woke up this morning
a little late.

Hurried
to shave and cut himself.

Hurried to eat breakfast
and hurried making
coffee (burned his hand).

Hurried to the car
and broke speed limits
getting to work.

Worked all day
trying to get everything
done by deadline.

Hurried home to
be on time for
dinner.

Hurried through
dinner to watch
T.V.

Fell asleep
watching T.V.
and went to
bed.

I watched
a butterfly today
flapping its wings;

Doing its work –
no hurry, just purpose.

What a lovely sight!
But I don't
have much time to
watch butterflies.

DREAM

For a very short period
of my life I actually
lived a dream.

The dream was one in
which I could fly.
I was free from
the Earth.

In my life I once
awoke from
heaviness and despair

And spent each
day marveling at
the wonders
around me.

Nothing was too small
to give me pleasure,
even ants on the pavement.

This continued for a
while. My friends asked
if I was taking drugs.

My heart was free
and giving was done
freely without mind.

I wish I knew how
to return to that time.

The Sage
smiles when
I tell him this.

"You have this
state within," he
whispers – "You
need only
    let
        go!"

THE UNITED STATES OF AMERICA

A good salesman who
wants you to try
his product

Will demonstrate.

He will show you the
virtues and win your
confidence.

He may even let you
try it.

His demeanor is calm;
his message clear and
he has no threats.

Everything about him
speaks of trust and
confidence

And in time
you will probably
buy his product.

Things that never
work for a salesman
are fear, anger and threats;

We would simply
go elsewhere.

Let us remember
this as we enter
this new market place.

MY BEST FRIENDS

My best friends I don't
see too often.

I know this sounds
strange but there's a reason.

For my heart to
resonate with another

There must be a
common chord

And this is in my
innermost heart;

All the rest is
window dressing.

And we know well
fair-weather friends.

I saw a friend
yesterday I hadn't
seen in a year.

It was as if we'd
never parted.

There was no
separation.

This unity is a
singular grace
from God.

DETERMINATION

We don't often think of it
as spiritual;

We prefer loftier
words.

But without it
there is no progress.

To reach the goal
of life can be a
long journey –

So easy to begin,
so easy to stop.

What is it that
keeps us going?

We don't think
of it as mystical;

Yet, what great
works come
without it?

Watch the salmon
swim upstream

And the beaver
building his dam.

Watch the snow goose
travel home.

They all
have this quality.

What has
happened in
our world?

What has
become of our
strong partner?

ARCH

An arch is such
a lovely curve;

But make no
mistake, it is
very strong.

Each brick placed
at an angle

Strengthens the
whole structure.

Ingenious, powerful
and graceful.

The Sage tells us
that good qualities
are from God.

Patience, tolerance,
love and faith are
bricks the Master Mason
hands us to put
into place.

If we do this
correctly the arch
of our life will
stretch to heaven.

MINKIE

Minkie the wonder
dog would
run all day.

I mean it.

As long as there
was a ball to
chase
she would run
till she died,

Without a thought
of dinner or sleep.

Always bringing
it back to her master.

Sometimes
the ball lands
in deep grass;
but Minkie
always finds
it, wherever!
You can count on it.

Have we
found it
or have we
given up?

There's a
lot to learn
from this
dog.

ALEXANDER

The innocence of this
baby was a joy to behold.

Then came the endless
wonder of childhood.
What is the next stage:
Is there something
inside that
doesn't change?

The body grows and
the mind expands.

Many things are
learned.

One day he is
an adult.

I wonder if the
Maker still sees
that innocence
in him – that
pure joy and trust.

These are
God's gifts.
We must be careful
not to lose them.

If we start
early enough we can
polish them
each day

So they never
fade.

This is a difficult
task, but what
else is there?

ECHOES

The first time I
heard an echo

I was a child; I
loved itl.

Everything I shouted
came back.

I wondered at first
who was there

And then I
knew it was me.

But still it was
intriguing.

And now there's
no echo anymore.

Or perhaps we just
don't hear.

The kind word and
acts are sent forth;

There is an echo,
only this one's invisible.

It comes back as
goodness and enters
the heart.

I love this feeling
just like when I
was young.

SLEEP

I'm finding there's
a difference between sleep
and torpor.

Sleep comes when the
body and mind are truly
tired.

Torpor says, "I'm here.
Don't you feel
tired? Take a nap."

It's like a false fuel
gauge that tells you
you're empty.

But if you knock it
hard the needle
bounces to full.

It takes a lot of
faith and determination
to reject torpor.

We've been brought
up to feel well rested;
this is our right.

What am I to do
with this imposter?
Time to get up.

TEA

I learned something new
today about making
tea.

If the pot boils briefly
and you pour into the
tea leaves

The result is delicious.

But if you let the pot
boil longer
there is
little flavor in the tea.

When the water is ready
use it at the right
time -- if we wait
we won't have a good cup.

God gives us these
moments of opportunity
that are
just right.

There's something inside
that says, do it right
now.

If we listen
with a true ear
the taste is
amazing

The window is open
only a few seconds.
We must remember.

SPOTLESS

I watched the Sage
and what he wore.
Usually it was white
and spotless.

If he took off a shirt
he never wore it
again till it
was washed.

He was spotless in
his dress, his
speech and his heart.

Well, we could start
with dress. Maybe
if we got that right
we could move to heart.

I usually say, Oh I
only wore it a few hours;
it's not dirty enough
to launder.

Each morning could
be my laundry time.

If I take all bad
memories, thoughts or
fears and toss them
in the machine

I will come out
spotless – ready for
work.

TRICKS

I put a little oil on
my razor blade
after shaving.

One blade will
last two months
this way.

Before it was
rusty in a week.

I get a lot of fun
out of seeing
how long this shiny
blade will last.

There are a lot of
tricks like
this that
surprise us.

Kindness is this way,
when I add it to
my speech with
others.

The face
stays pure and
open.
There is no
place for sadness
and fear.

Maybe I'm
onto something!

MY ELBOW

I have a bad
elbow.

It's fine most of the
time, but if I use
it in a certain way
it is painful.

My doctor says it's
the little fascia
which line the muscle
to the bone.

They tear and
create layer
fissures.

I tried everything
but found no
relief.

Then I stopped
using my arm to
do the little things
that pained it.

My arm has started
to heal – I can feel it.

It's very simple –I don't
do the thing that
hurts the tissue. I refrain.

I used to tease a friend;
she always got angry.
Now I've stopped
doing this and our
whole friendship
has blossomed.

Is it really this simple?

HASTINESS

I'm often in a hurry.
I just like to get
things done – quickly.

The other day I knocked
over a bottle in my
hastiness.

I got angry at
the bottle first,
blaming it for
being in the
wrong place.

Then I got
angry at myself –
the real culprit.

This is a funny
thing.

I'm not perfect;
I make mistakes.
I can forgive others
but not myself.

When will I learn,
forgiveness
begins at home just
like charity.

It certainly will make
my life calmer.
And anger,
the stranger
outside, won't
come to my
door.

PENMANSHIP

When I was in
first grade I won
prizes for my penmanship.

I formed letters so
gracefully – they were
works of art.
I took pride in doing them
well.

But things have changed.
Sometimes now I
write so fast I can't
read my writing.

What happened to
the child who loved
to form a letter?

He's still there just
watching.

I slowed down the
other day, and found to
my amazement I
could write beautifully.

So much to do, so
little time. But isn't
this where all the
problems begin?

SEX

It's just like an
itch that needs
to be scratched.

You scratch it and
it's fine for a
while.

Then it itches again
and you begin
all over.

I once let it itch
until it stopped;
it didn't come
back.

They say sex is
the only thing
you want till
you have it.

Isn't it strange
how molehills
become mountains
so quickly.

THE MIRROR

Did you ever look
at yourself in the mirror?

Not how you look but
what you are.

The eyes tell it all.

Try it sometime. If
you look intently into
those eyes

Your conscience awakens
and might tell you
some interesting things.

These messages
are unflinching:

You will know
immediately your
state.

You might
see the difference
from a year ago.

Progress is slow
but steady if we
use this mirror
daily.

POETRY

I can't get this
poetry out of my
system.

I don't even know
if it's poetry.

But each morning
it bubbles up

And I write.

Later on I read
it. I say to
myself,

Not bad – did
I really write that?

If we let the heart
pour forth

We are bound to get
some pebbles.
But look at
these other
stones:

How precious they are;
How they sparkle.

HERE TODAY

I know I'll be
gone in a little
while.

We all go.

I feel some sense
of urgency but
mostly I watch.

I know I need
that special sense

That comes from
the center
of my heart.

It sees through the
filter of God

And places each
thing in its
proper place.

Eternity in a grain
of sand always
sounded good.

I'm beginning
to see how it's
possible.

TREES

I love trees. They
have always seemed
part of my life.

They give me shade
in summer and as
a child I used to
play in their branches.

Now, the scientists
tell us how good they
are for pollution.

Trees have this
wondrous gift of taking
in bad and giving out good.

The Sage did this
even in his sleep.

We watched it happen
daily

And we all felt
bathed in this
pure air.

Our pollution was
absorbed; for a
while our faults vanished.

But we are saplings,
are we not?
Do we know our
own power?

THE DOG

Each morning on my
walk I encounter a
large black dog.

He is behind a
wire fence.

Often he is sleeping,
but awakened
he barks at me.

This morning I
stopped near him
as he barked and growled.

I said a prayer over
and over and the
strangest thing happened –

He stopped barking.

Then he looked afraid
and started backing away.

Finally he turned
and trotted off.

The power of God
is this way:

It dispels fear and
deepens faith.

With it we can
do anything;

Without it, the
dog will keep barking.

Part Three

WHAT IS IT?

What is it that
holds us back?

When we are about to try,
what is it that stops us?

When we see the good,
what is it that hides it?

When we sense another's pain,
what is it that lets us walk by?

When we pray,
what is it that scatters our mind?

When we surrender,
what gives us second thoughts?

When we find what it is
we have begun.

THE PATH

Standing on the plain, the wise
man pointed to the left.

As far as the eye could see
were pastures, rivers and meadows.

Then he turned to the right
and looked up.

A steep mountain climbed into
the clouds, and a narrow
winding path disappeared
above.

On the left is Hell, he said,
and this path on the right
leads to Heaven.

The meadows are pleasant, the
fruit is tasty.

But above the wind howls
and our hands are chilled.

Better hurry – the
Sage is already climbing.

WALKING

The country road winds
along a ridge.

Sunlight filters through
the trees.

To each side are valleys
stretching for miles.

It is a pleasant walk
through the light and shadows.

But we can't forget
why we are walking.

Where did we start;
where will we finish?

Our mind cannot walk,
only our legs.

Who is doing the walking?
Who is moving?

HUMILITY

I am probably the most
humble person of anyone
I know, said the T.V. star.
And he believed it.

This is the treachery
of the ego. It tells
us we have none.

The Sage tells us
the more we practice
humility the more
our true exaltedness
is seen.

But most of us don't
want to die before
we die; and this
is the only path to
humility.

When God goes I am there;
when I go, God is there.
But when I go, I die.

SURRENDER

"Just let go and jump;
I'll catch you,"
said my father.

And trusting him
I did, and my fear
vanished
into my trust.

There is a story of a
man clinging to a
root on a cliff.

He prayed to God
for help and the
answer came,
"Let go."

Looking down into
black space he
swallowed and fell.

An instant later he
landed in a garden

And found fruits
of unimaginable taste.

It is this way, said
the Sage.
What you lose is
that which
keeps you bound.

So with this
whispered
advice I let go —
and drop
into God.

THE LITTLE BOY

Eyes so blue you
can see into
the Soul.

A smile so light
it brings joy
to the heart.

At one second a
man can be a
saint, the next
a devil;

And so it is
with the little
boy.

He simply unrolls
the scroll of his
life, his karma.

He mimics what
he has seen, for
he has no sin.

He is God's gift
to his parents.
He is a reminder
of his Father.

FORGIVENESS

It is said that when
we have been wronged
we should ask forgiveness
from the doer.

"How ridiculous," said
I – "and how unfair.
Justice isn't like
that."

But, forgiveness lives
in its own land – one
untraveled by most
pilgrims.

To understand it
we must practice
it – slaying the
dragons of anger
and fear.

Only then will we
know in a second
the sweetness, the
freedom that lies
inside.

THE TAILOR

I sat up late one
night looking down
into the window
of a tailor.

He labored quietly
under the dull light
of a lantern.

His face was a
study of focus
and peace.

Se saw not the
hours and heard
not the noises
from the street.

His one master
was duty and
in it he was
at one with himself.

No need to ask him
his wage or his
profit – these came
effortlessly.

He stopped for a
second and looked up
as if to remember something,

Then went quietly back
to his work.

THE DOG

My dog waits for me
at the gate each night
when I come home.
He is always there.

Whenever I call him
he comes running,
eager to lick
his master's hand.

Such loyalty I have
rarely seen in
humans.
It seems we always
want something
for our efforts.

God gave us each
creation to teach us.
But what will
we do with our
knowledge?

Our master
is calling: Isn't
it time we
ran to Him?

NIGHT BLOOMING SIRIUS

One night in Japan
my Japanese host
knocked on my door.

"Come quickly," he said.
"It is happening now."

I went into his
house and sitting on
the floor was
his whole family.

They were watching
the Sirius unfold.

"It only does this
one night a year,"
my host said.

The perfume in
the room was
fragrant.

All eyes, all hearts
focused on the
blossom.

Such a rare happening
that evening:
the flower and
the unity.

FAULTS

It is said whatever fault
we see in another
lies within ourselves.

"How can this be so?"
I say, righteous to
a fault.

I'm not greedy, I'm
not resentful, I'm
not judgmental

But take what is
mine, what has been
hard won.

And quickly my
peace turns to
indignation.

I have a right to
be indignant,
say I – look what
I've lost.

The wise man
listened to me and
said, "But you
never owned it,
my son. It has
all been given to us."

Oh my father,
when will I learn?

THE ANT

Did you ever hear an
ant complain?

Work, work, work,
endlessly struggle

Clear the debris,
bury the dead

Feed the commune,
perform duty:

What a lesson
for us mortals.

Were we to do
one day what
the ant does
every day

We might see
We might understand

And then know that
we must become
ants ourselves.

THE FUNERAL (It's too late then)

But he died so suddenly.
No one was prepared.
No one is ever prepared.

I had some things to
tell him. I'm sorry
he's gone now.

There was the good
and the bad. The bad
sometimes overshadowed
the good.

In each of us is that
sweetness of soul.
What a shame we
don't see it.

We know it's there but
it's obscured by the
shadows.

And now the shadows
have claimed the
body and the soul
has gone on.

We should learn from
death. It must be
done now, today. Don't
wait – sweetness is yours.

SNOW GEESE

Snow geese mate forever;
they never change partners.

If one dies the other
does not remarry.

They live their lives
this way in loyalty,
trust and duty.

Wherever they go
they go in unity.

Why is it we
struggle so hard
in marriage?

Certainly God has
given us direction
and grace.

As the snow goose
flies unerringly to
his destination,

So do we need
that compass which
directs our efforts.

Unity is when two
hearts are one, and
merging with God
is the same.

SEEDS

The more things change
the more they stay
the same.

A caterpillar carries
within it the butterfly
germ.

An acorn carries
within the mighty
oak.

And we, what
do we carry
within?

What is our heritage,
what is our
potential?

Do we know this.
Do we care.
Do we understand.

What can I do
to nourish this
seed?

The rain falls on
all things – weeds
and vegetables alike.

But the vegetables
grow into useful
forms. How about
me?

HUMMINGBIRD

I watched a hummingbird
the other day.
Its wings moved
faster than my eyes.

It hovered and drank
the nectar and
moved on to the
next bloom –
faster than a wink.

It knew exactly
where to put its
tongue,
where to find
sweetness.

I wish I were
like the hummingbird.
What a life – finding
sweetness everywhere.

"But there is sweetness
everywhere," said
the Sage. "You
must recognize the
fragrance first."

The sweetness that
nourishes comes in
a thousand forms.
Start moving,
wings.

A DOG

Even dogs know
about God.

The other morning
very early I was
doing prayers.

The holy place I
was in was
lit with light.

At the end of
my meditation
I saw a movement
outside.

When I looked
closer, I saw a
small white dog
shivering in the dawn.

He put his paws
on the glass and
leaned, looking in.

A magnet
draws metal filings.
Those with open hearts
are also drawn in –
to the light.

CLEANING THE POT

I have a copper pot.
It's pretty when
it's clean but often
I neglect it, doing
other things.

Then I see its state
and set about to
polish it. In a
short time it is
gleaming.

A clean pot shows
its beauty – shows
its true color – a
gold red luster.

We are like this:
Unless we polish
every day we become
tarnished, neglected.

But gold needs
no effort to enhance
its beauty. It
shows its value in
an instant.

It is said that
in ancient times
the alchemist could
change copper to gold.

We have a master Alchemist!

THE FOOT RACE

In a foot race
someone has to
win. How sad
for the losers.

Wouldn't it
be something if
all the racers
agreed to tie?

What a sight at
the finish line:
seven runners absolutely
in unity,

Even thwarting
the electronic timer
which broke because
it could not decide.

What a wonder;
people would
talk about it
for a long time.

This a long
foot race we're
in. Let's see
what we can do.

GETTING THERE IS THE FUN

After you I
insist. No I
insist, after you.
Who goes first?

The first shall
be last and
the last shall
be first, we are told.

We can tell a
lot about a person
from the way
he drives.

Even a saint
will run a
red light
sometimes.

We need to get
there as fast as
possible, we argue.

What is it they say
about army life?
Hurry up and wait.

In olden days, a
carriage pulled by
four white horses was
quite a sight.
      It still is
if we slow down to see it.

THE CARVER

As a child, I
watched in awe as
my father carved
an animal from a
block of wood.

At first I thought it
would be a dog, but
as the shavings fell
I saw it was an
eagle.

I picture it now
perched on my
dresser. But then
in my mind's eye
it soared high
above the Earth.

There is a big difference
between an eagle and
a vulture. One
is very noble.

We have wings now
with feathers. We
can fly. Why
are we still hopping
about down here,
looking for carrion?

DON'T BITE A DOG

Somehow, not
meaning to, I had
enraged the
driver behind me.

He cut in front
of me, narrowly
missing my
fender. He
was furious and
ready to fight.
What was I to do?

I could see the
headlines: Motorist
beats motorist with
jack iron.

Our ego is
our worst enemy. It
tells us: Go ahead,
you're right.

When an angry
dog bites you, do you
bite back?
I walk away
these days. Better
one little scar than
a broken skull.

The wise man understands
that anger is the
father of sin. Thank
God for
patience.

MAKING TEA

FIRST there is the dry
tea, then the
hot water and sugar and
milk.

We mix them together
for a few minutes and
we have a lovely
hot cup of tea.

Somewhere along the
way each ingredient
gives up its flavor
to the whole.

The United Nations is
quite a cup of tea.
Each country, color,
ethnos is put
into the pot.

Hopefully the taste
is good – if someone
didn't put in too
much sugar or tea.

What each element
can provide is amazing.
It loses its individuality
to enhance the flavor
of the tea.

What must I
do then? What flavor
can I make?

BALANCE

The tourist curses the rain;
the farmer welcomes it.

The sunbather loves the
hot sun.
The crops wither under
its glare.

Ice and snow cause many
accidents.
But in the spring
they change to water
filling the reservoirs.

What are we to do
with all this?

Wherein lies the
balance, the
meaning?

In my adolescence
I was devastated by
my failures.

Now, looking
back I see their value.

Can we fast-forward
to understand
our present misfortune?
I hope so.

COMPOST

Everything has a value,
even the excrement
of a worm.

Soil experts tell us
there is no soil
like it.

And from this soil
grows the tastiest
fruits and herbs;

And when they die
they return as
food for the worm.

So even dirt has
a real value in
God's world.

And what of our
sins and faults –
what is their value?

If we compost them
they might provide
us with something
useful.

WHAT WE HAVE

Before two travelers began
a journey they sought
advice from a Sage.

The one who asked if
it was a good day to
travel was told "yes,"

while the one who
asked if it was a bad
day was told "no."

It's all in how we
see things. The
glass is really
half full or half
empty.

The poor troubadour
sitting on the curb
sang of having no
shoes.

When he looked across
the street he saw
a man who had
no legs.

A poor man
once prayed
to God for
help. He
later found a small
lump of gold
under his bed.

Unhappy, he
asked why had
God not given
him a larger hunk.

God,
help us to love
what we have,
not to have
what we love.

MORNING WALK

On my morning walk
I rounded a curve
and came
upon an old dog
resting in the middle
of the road.

He raised his head a
little to watch me walk
by. I thought he would
bark – all the others did.

But this dog was old,
getting ready to leave.
Perhaps he had seen
enough not to bark.

It was a strange silence
between us. It
must be nice to arrive at
that point in life.

Accepting the things that
pass by without judging,
and lowering our head
to rest a bit -- this seems
like a good start.

MY FINGER

One day I lost the tip of
my finter.

I wasn't looking
the accident came
and it was gone.

I have a friend
who is losing toes.

What lesson in
all this?

We don't own our
body – it's a gift.

Finally, the whole
body will be taken.

Thank God for my
small lesson.

It's time to look
at what's real.

QUICKSILVER

Did you ever play
with quicksilver?

I remember as a
child, separating it
on a table.

But it didn't like
that and flowed
back together.

If we take the
colors of the rainbow

And trace them back
to their source

They come from a
prism of pure light.

In that prism
there are no colors.

What about us?
Don't we see the
prism?

It's time to
retrace our steps.

There's a unity
inside which
has no differences.

GETTING ANGRY

I always thought
it was the things
in the world that
made me angry.

Then one day in
the kitchen I
stubbed my toe.
I was furious.

There was no one
around to blame,
nothing to yell at:

Only myself and
the villain anger
who had stepped
out of his inner box.

Is this what the
Sage meant when*
he said the
war is inside?

Now I know
who my enemy
is. He's no
longer out there.

THE OYSTER

Far beneath the sea
the oyster meditates
on a piece of sand
inside its shell.

With care and over
time the sand
becomes a pearl
of great beauty.

Everything in God's
creation is a lesson.
Where is our
grain of sand, then?

We need something
with which to
work.

How about mistakes?
If we make enough
we might have a
grain.

What can be built
around this
imperfection?

Understanding and
Patience, and duty
have the glow
of a pearl.

THE FIG TREE

On my way home
this morning

I stopped by a fig
tree heavy with fruit.

Some had already
fallen and were rotting.

But many remained
green and ripe on the tree.

I picked six – soft in
my hand as they came free.

There was no charge;
the tree gave freely.

It's simply what the
fig tree does:

It never asks for praise
and never changes.

What figs have I
to give?

The Sage says
we must serve others.

Why is it so
easy for the tree?

SKINS

The best part of a banana
is the fruit not the skin.

We never eat the
shell of a walnut.

Carefully we extract
the sweet nut.

When my friend
gets angry with me

I see only his shell;
I easily forget the nut inside.

The wise man sees
the sweet fruit in each of us;

He is not looking
at the cover.

When will I
learn the value of
a human being?

Our fruit is
covered over.

We should peel it
before it spoils.

SALT

You can taste
the difference a pinch
of salt makes.

The latent flavors
in the food
emerge.

My father gave
me a word of
praise once.

It still lies within;
when I taste it
I try to do better.

Give a horse a
lump of sugar,
he'll jump through
hoops.

Think of the power
of a kind word.
It can change
a life.

INCENSE

Incense, unless
burned, has no
flavor.

Isn't this a
wonder – it has
to die to perform
its duty.

Fruits' only purpose
is to be eaten.
What a wonder:
Just when you're
most beautiful
you are eaten.

When do we reach
our ripeness, and
what happens to
it?

Are we then like
the fruit? Must
we be consumed?
Is this the purpose
of our life?

Sitting in the
corner, the Sage
is nodding his head.

THE CHILD KNOWS

When I was a
child and I could see,
my heart
understood each face.

There was a goodness inside
which sought
only to
serve others.

There was no veil
between my life and
my friends; their sorrow
was mine.

All of this happened
without seeking,
without explanation,
without effort.

Why then now
do I struggle
with these things?

The same child
is within.

Each act, each
thought, each deed
of ignorance
keeps this child
locked inside.

LET GO

The Sage told us
what we love
in this world will
destroy us.

In Asia they put
fruit in a gourd
with a narrow neck.

The monkey
reaches in, grabs
the fruit, and won't
let go. His fist is
too wide to come
out and the farmer
catches him.

Monkey, monkey, just
let go – that fruit
surely isn't worth
your life.

Smoking will be the
death of me, said the
sick man as he
lit another.

The Sage reminds us
it is time to stop
acting like animals.
They don't know any
better.

What is the link between
wanting and doing?
Doing requires
certitude.

HUMILITY

The more you make
yourself humble and
ask for forgiveness the
more your true
exaltedness is seen.

These words of the
Sage ring clear in
my heart and I
set out to do my
best.

But someone
is rude to me
and I just can't
resist getting even.

Surely there
must be another way,
one that doesn't
require vanishing.

I watched a child
blow up a balloon.
It got so big and
pop! It was gone.

Either way we
vanish – only
one makes no
noise and has
no death.

IMAGE

What we see on a movie
screen is an image.
We may take it as
real.

But, the
only real thing
is the screen
on which the
images dance.

All the rest is
illusion. We
love illusion – our
minds rise to
the occasion.

Embellishing, judging,
blaming and wanting,
We are ready to
trade wisdom
for pleasure.

Underneath the
images the screen
rests silently. It
knows when the light
is gone it will remain.

Wouldn't it be a
great thing to discover
the thing inside of us
that remains after
the mind goes?

TRAVELER

The wise traveler
begins his journey
with many bags
and ends with none.

Our wants are
far greater than
our needs and
much louder.

They keep shouting,
give me this,
give me that.
They are imposters
wearing needs' clothes.

I saw a man in a
restaurant angry
because his soup
was cold – while
outside a child
was starving.

Buddhists say
all suffering comes
from desires.

I have so many
wants. Would
you carry them
for me/?
They're quite
heavy.

THE TAIL

I watched my dog once
chasing his tail
in a circle.

He was very
earnest.

Even if I had told
him it was a
mistake

He wouldn't have stopped.

Around and around
I go, my tail
changing color and
form.

One minute it's
a book, the next
a woman and now
a gem.

If I give my dog
something tasty
he might stop.

What prize for me
would make
me stop running
and bring me home?

TIGER TAMING

I had a friend once
but he stopped saying hello.

Whatever I said he
would look away.

I thought it was me
but I had done no wrong,

So I stopped saying hello
for a while.

Until a small voice
said – this is wrong.

So I said hello again
with a smile.

One day he smiled
back and said hello.

One can tame a
tiger in time.

All it takes is
patience.

But first I have
to tame the
tiger inside.

THE ROOSTER

The rooster is the
first one to get
up for prayers.

He likes to tell
the world.

He doesn't really
have to get
up;

He has a very busy
day ahead
of him.

But he does it
anyway; it's
his duty.

He starts the day
before the day
starts with
a call and a prayer.

What wonders
God hath
wrought.

ENYATTA'S NECKLACE

Enyatta lost her
priceless necklace.

She had everyone in
the palace looking
for it.

She was desolate
for three days,

When a friend
noticed something
around her neck.

Is this what
you lost, she asked.

The necklace had
been there all
along.

The Sage tells us
God is always
within. So
isn't it time
we stopped searching?

THE GARLAND

Death comes when
we least expect it.

The Sage tells us
we wear the garland
of death around our
neck.

We just don't see it.

What is it made of,
this garland?

These are precious
gems of God's qualities
strung on a pure strand
of wisdom.

If we touch it
we can feel its
cool
smoothness.

It can change the
way we act. It
can bring us
to God.

LIGHT

If I get up in
the middle of the night
I will often stumble
over something.

Sometimes I even
become fearful
of something in
the room.

But as soon as I
switch on the light
I become peaceful.
All is in order.

If we are
without light we
can stumble and
be afraid.

It is this way
in our lives.

The Sage tells
us that the
light of God
is wisdom.

To truly see things in
perspective and the
true
value
of each action.

What a wondrous
light to switch
on! Then we
can be peaceful.

BAD DREAM

For many years I
had a bad dream.
I have it less now
but it still comes.

I am in college and
need a course to graduate.
But I refuse to go
to the course.

Each day of the class
I sit in my room
knowing I
won't graduate;

But still I don't go.
The dream troubled
me for I did not
understand.

Then the Sage told me:
"Your life is a university.
If you go to class,
make effort,
you will pass
the exam on Judgment Day."

Now that I understand I'm
doing better. I rarely have
the dream but I still
struggle with classes.
When will I graduate?

IDOL WORSHIP

We feel we have come
a long way since
the days of idol worship.

We are not heathens.
We say: We know
about God and worship Him.

But church time may
interfere with our
favorite T.V. show.

Who wins?

When we have a spare
moment we can
read books of wisdom.
But we have a magazine.

Who wins?

At a wedding when we
talk with an old lady
our eyes go to the
young virgin dancing.

Who wins?

My wife needs house
repairs done but
I have music to
listen to and games
to play.

Who wins?

I know that
I have come a
long way from
idol worship.

How about you?

THE BUMBLEBEE

Bzzz-Bzzz – I hear
him long before I
see him.

I even know what
he's doing before
I see him.

There he is, a
golden blur of wings
and movement,

Moving faithfully
from flower to
flower.

He doesn't waste time;
there is important
work to do.

If only I had half
the energy, I
say.

But what would
I do with it?

Would I labor
without lunch
break – finding
nectar in each
crevice?

Would I be
as one-pointed
as he?

FLYING

I sometimes have a
dream about flying.

My way of flying is
to move my arms rapidly

And slowly I begin
to hover aloft.

It is wondrous and
it seems so natural.

I pinch myself to
see if I'm awake.

When I have
traveled a distance

I alight and then
wake up.

"My God," say I.
"That was something!"

The Sage tells
us in olden days

People with great faith
did this regularly

Without engines
or wings.

In this modern age
of technology

We can't
conceive of this.

Our teacher, Science,
tells us one thing.

Our father tells
us another.

MEDICINES

What medicine do I
need for my heart?

It is always ill
at ease.
What pill can I take
to calm my mind?

Oh I know there are
all these drugs,

But they only work
for a while

And they change the
way I feel.

Indians in the
jungle have cures from
a common herb.

They work beautifully
and are free
if you know where
to find them.

The Indian
grinds his herb,
mixes
and prepares it
with skill.

Patience is a powerful
potion.

It could cure
many illnesses;

But in its raw
form it is useless.

It needs
preparation – faith,
certitude and determination –
to prosper;
and that takes patience.

But do I
have the patience
to prepare it?

FAITH

How can something
help me that I
can't see, touch, hear
or even know?

If a medieval man
entered our world he
would be awestruck
by electricity.

The things we
take for granted –
T.V., radio, microwaves –
would be miracles to him.

No matter how we
tried to explain
them, he couldn't
understand.

Someone came
long before us and
gave us these
things.

If He tried
to explain the
mysteries of our
life to us
we wouldn't understand.

And if he said,
You needn't understand,
just have faith

A few of us might listen.

WOODWORKING

A carpenter will choose
a good piece of wood
to work with.

He has in mind
a finished product.

In the beginning it
is heavy work
chopping and cutting

And gradually when
he sees the form
take place

The work becomes
more painstaking.

At this point, mistakes
are difficult to
repair.

In the beginning we
are unshaped.

And then we are born.

As a child we
take form quickly;
growth is fast.

But as we
get older – the
work requires
more care.

Wisdom must
become analytic
and finally divine.

Even small words
can hurt
the heart.
We must be
careful carpenters.

BEATING AN ORANGE

A fool and a wise man
walked in an orange grove.
Both were hungry.

The fruits were lovely
but still unripe.

The fool eagerly
grabbed a
fruit which was hard,

And to make it
soft he pounded
it against a rock.

When it was soft
he ate it, only to
discover it was bitter.

The wise man smiled
and walked on knowing
the time would come.

The Sage tells us,
there is a time for
each thing.

Often I get
impatient, frustrated
because my child
can't see the truth.

No matter how much
I lecture – there
is no change.

I forgot that
at that age
I was the same.

The Tao Te Ching
tells us:
"The Noble man
changes slowly
like a lion –
never trust sudden
change."

We should not
judge the caterpillar
too soon – give
it time.

OUTER CHURCH

Yesterday I walked
inside a huge
cathedral,

Its pillars of
marble and colored
windows,

The beams soaring
to a ceiling far
above the crowd.

My friend said:
How much labor
and money it cost to build.

Some people in
front were praying
just as I do at home.

I wonder, would
my prayer be
better in here?

God gives us the
outer church until
we have the inner.

FRAGRANCE

You don't have
to tell a bee
where to find a flower.

It goes directly
there guided by
the fragrance.

Some people I
seek out: I just
like their company.

What we are
speaks louder
than what we say.

This inner fragrance
is in all people
but only a few display it.

What is their secret?
How do they mine
their sweetness?

The Sage tells us,
see the truth as
Goodness and put this
into action.

This fragrance,
this goodness is the
fruit of our actions.

RIVERS

Some rivers rush
directly to the
sea;

Others meander
through the countryside,
taking their time
as they wander.

The first is good
for a fast
journey.

But more and more
I like the
scenery.

Anyway, my
old engine won't
push me any faster.

Hopefully it will
take me all the
way.

Oh God, you
created this old
stream.

Please guide
it to the sea.

BIRD NESTS

Did you ever watch
a bird build a nest?
It's a wonder.

So many trips to and
fro, so much pecking
and nudging.

Finally it is in
place.

If you take it
apart you will see
its art.

We could never do
it in a hundred
years.

All God's creations
have their
skills and tasks.

If this is the
bird's, what is
ours?

What has
God given us
to do that no
bird can do?

What nest need
we build?

The Sage tells
us we must create
our house in
heaven while
we're here.

I'd better find some
sticks quickly
before winter
comes.

FISHING

The fisherman rows
to a spot on the lake
and puts out his lines.

He waits:
Each hour he shifts his lines
and waits.

Towards sunset
there is movement
on one line.

He still waits.
After a bit the
line moves to one side,

And the old man
moves with the speed
of a cat.

He jerks the line
and soon he has
a silver prize
in his boat,

Long, long
before the younger
fishermen have
returned to the village.

In our lives
it's like this:
We must know
where the
prize lies.

We must
go there
each day.

We must
be attentive
and
very
patient.

And we
must act quickly
when the
time is right.

We'll have enough
food for the
whole village.-

THE THERAPIST

I saw a therapist for years.
I felt a little better
each time I left his office.

But not for long.
The old fears came back.

You know the saying,
it's the blind leading the blind?

Well, I understand this
now about my old therapist.

I found out later
he had his own therapist.

I finally found
a master therapist.

He told me,
Life isn't so much
a problem to be solved
but to be understood.

If I understand
I can accept.

If I accept I
have some peace.

With peace comes
learning and unity.

Why didn't I
find this man earlier?

WASHING MACHINES

Washing machines are
wonderful – they
do all the work for us.

Just throw in the
clothes, set the dial
and relax.

I'm an old
garment with a lot
of stains.

I could use a
washing machine
to remove these spots.

I found one once
several years ago
but I didn't use it.

I wasn't sure it would
work and I didn't want
to waste my coins.

Something
has happened: I use
this machine every day now.

I can hardly see the
stains. If I
keep using it,
I think they'll vanish.

To use this
machine you
have to put
yourself inside

And be tumbled:
It tosses you
around a bit.

But look how
I am when
I come out.
It's worth the effort.

Practicing
good qualities
is never easy.

COVERS

They say you can't
tell a book by its cover.
How true.

What about people?

Covers tend to wear
out over time.

What are we left
with?

Only the lines and pages and
what is written on them.
Now we're getting closer.

What you are speaks
louder than what you say.

I have a friend who
talks a blue streak.

He's a rather odd-
looking person too.

When I was sick, he
was the only one
who came.

He brought soup and
a lot more.

He showed me his
wiser pages.

KITES

No matter how high my
kite goes, it's still connected
to the Earth.

Almost invisible but
there's a long string.

What would happen
if I cut it?

What would the kite do?
Where would it go,
how would it feel?

It must be wonderful
to be as free as that.

Soaring endlessly about:
no ties to the Earth.

The Sage tells us
the true man is free.

I think, though, that
he also has a tether

But that line is
anchored above.

MOVIE HOUSE

Did you ever notice
how your finger
stops hurting when
you go to the movies?

For two hours you
forget it but after you
come out, it
begins to throb again.

Isn't there a
movie house I could
spend my life in to
remove my pain?

The Sage tells us
there is: The problem
is we have to build
it, brick by brick.

I've started but
there's a long way to go.
Yet sometimes already
when I sit in it I
can feel my troubles go.

I can't wait till
it's finished.

THE WELL

When the water
first comes from the
well it may be dirty.

There are rust and impurities
that have gathered in
the pipe.

But soon we will
see pure water flowing
out.

On my morning walk
my knee always aches
for the first five minutes.
Then the pain goes.

When I sit to meditate
my mind is crazy;
it just won't stop.

But if I have patience
all this will go away,
replaced by a gentle calm.

If Spring stopped
trying, we'd never
have Summer.

SNIPPING

When I was younger
each
month I went
to the barbershop.

The quiet snipping
sound, the careful
attention the barber
gave to his client,

These things
were so peaceful I
would be lulled
into sleep.

And sometimes when
my wife is occupied
with a small task

Her focus and
quiet attentiveness
will calm me and
make me drowsy.

If we have
clarity we can
sense the care of
the master
doing small duties
around us.

It is so peaceful
when I feel this;
I may fall
asleep again.

MY FRIEND

Once in New York
something strange
happened:

I LET GO!

My life had been in
black and white
and suddenly
it became color.

I do not know,
to this day, why
or what happened.

I only know that
my old companion,
worry, went on
vacation.

My strength doubled;
I saw into minds.
Each day was a
birthday.

I dared not tell
a soul – for I knew
the telling would
scare this new friend away.

When did he leave
me, this friend?
How can I find
him again?

UNDERSTANDING

I don't feel like
writing poetry this
morning.

My wife is ill.
It's like I am
too.

I don't like it
but this is the way
it should be.

Every pain of our
fellow human being
should be ours.

The cynic says, but
I'm separate – why
whould I have her pain?

It's not that I get
sick, it's that my
heart understands her pain.

And with this open
heart I am able to
receive help and grace.

Without it I am
closed off. My
garden is
covered with plastic
and the plants can't
grow.

INSTINCT

Sometimes
on certain tropical isles
small crabs begin an exodus
from the beach inland
to a higher place.

They have an instinct that
tells them to travel a
certain distance. It is an
arduous journey.

Then the typhoon comes
and washes to within a few
yards of these crabs.
They are safe.

How did they know
the storm was coming
days before
it arrived?

How did they know how
far to travel, and what
gave them the certitude
to do this march?

Squirrels save for
the winter – wise
farmers put away
extra grain.

And we as God's
children. What
do we put away?
Have we begun
our exodus?

We all know
the storm is
coming. What
then keeps us
from acting?

Every creation
of God is
used as a lesson.
Perhaps we
should open
the book.

THE COVER

It is a simple truth:
the kingdom of
heaven lies within.

That the part of the
fruit most sweet
is inside.

If we discard the
outer covering we
discover the fragrance.

Our lives are often
consumed by the
covering.

We analyze it.
We dissect it and
we worship it.

But it's only a
covering.
That is its
purpose, to cover.

The sweet section
has its duty too:
to nourish and please.

The Sage
was like this. He had
no outer
covering.

When I was
around him, I
breathed a fragrance.

There was
no trouble,
no pain – I had
come home.

WHITE

I love the color
white. It is
pure and clean.

In Italy men
wear white.

White is the
brilliance of the sun.

Other colors
have personality;

White has none.

Everything can
go along with
white – it doesn't
clash or choose.

You can draw on
it clearly.

But the problem
is – you need
to wash it often
for it to
stay white.

AIRPLANES

Air travel is usually
smooth – but
sometimes there is
turbulence.

Unannounced,
the plane drops like
a stone
and rises suddenly.

We are helpless
victims caught
in the play of
nature.

Terror is in the
eyes of passengers,
except one.

Across the
aisle is a small
child
delighted by the cosmic
roller coaster.

We wish it
would cease – he,
reveling in God's play,
wants more.

When did
we lose that
innocent joy
and faith?

The Sage
tells us it is
ours for
the asking.

MIMOSA

A certain kind
of mimosa is of
delicate design.

If you brush
against it, it
will close –

And stay that
way till
danger is past.

Some people
are this way,
with very fragile
emotions.

What may
roll off our skin
may
penetrate them.

The Sage says
that even not to
hurt another
is a good life.

THE KEY

Locked in a dark box
   we can see the light outside.
The key lies next to us
   and we imagine using it.
But the darkness enthralls
   and we rest motionless.

In our world of dreams
   we can see freedom.
In our world of dreams
   we see pictures
so beautiful we can cry.
Yet they remain
     as pictures
without taste, or nourishment.
Is this our Destiny?

The wise ones came.
   They showed us light.
We understood,
   if only fleetingly.

They told us
where the key was
and how to use it.
And still we sit,
   waiting.

As human beings
   we are children of God.
To grow we must
leave the darkness
   and fulfill our destiny.
Here is the key.
We must use it.
Now.

Once the door
   is open
we are flooded
   in light.
There is no
darkness or shadow.
We have
merged.

Other books by Locke Rush

The True Marriage: A Guidebook for a Lifelong Journey

"I just recently read the book three times in one day I enjoyed it so much. I am excited and making changes daily in my relationship, which are already beginning to create a healthier and more loving reelationship than I have had in over six years."

—MINDY FONTAINE, Schoolteacher, Steamboat Springs, Colorado

"I read your lovely little book, The True Marriage, last evening. You certainly hit the proverbial nail on the head. I especially resonate with the need for patience, compassion and love. This book would be perfect for marriage counselors to 'read' with their clients. It is gentle and probing rather than commandment-directed."

—ROY FAIRFIELD, Professor Emeritus, The Union Institute

Finding The Way Home

"My wife and I are both eading this book, we can't put it down. I've read a lot of spiritual auto biographies over the years and I must say this one is the most inspiring. It is alive."

—ZOHAIR, Virginia

"It's immensely readable. I find myself turning pages to find out what is going to be around the next bend in the author's path. The author has created a thrilling journey into his own consciousness—I've never read anything like it, and I think the author is on to something that will reach many lay people who will be interested in his story, will be able to relate to it, and will be led along to seek what he has found....I gave this wonderful book, which I have now finished, to my son. I plan to give it to at least four more people."

—SHIRLEY, Virginia

www.ingramcontent.com/pod-product-compliance
Lightning Source LLC
Chambersburg PA
CBHW061253110426
42742CB00012BA/1898